I0448360

TABLE OF CONTENTS

i

ACRONYMS

ADP	Army Doctrine Publication
ARNORTH	U.S. Army North
BCT	Brigade Combat Team
CAM	Combined Arm Maneuvers
CBP	Capabilities Based Assessment
CBRNE	Chemical Biological Radiological Nuclear Explosive
CERFP	CBRNE Enhance Response Force
CIA	Central Intelligence Agency
CJCS	Chairman of Joint Chief of Staff
CM	Consequence Management
CONPLAN	Contingency Plan
CST	Civil Support Team
DA	Decisive Action
DC	District of Columbia
DCE	Defense Coordinating Element
DCO	Defense Coordinating Officer
DCRF	Defense CBRNE Response Force
DHS	Department of Homeland Security
DIA	Defense Intelligence Agency
DOD	Department of Defense
DSCA	Defense Support of Civil Authorities
EXORD	Execution Order
FBI	Federal Bureau Investigation
FEMA	Federal Emergency Management Administration

FM	Field Manual
FY	Fiscal Year
GAO	Government Accountability Office
HD	Homeland
HRF	Homeland Response Force
HQ	Headquarters
IED	Improvised Explosive Device
JDOMS	Joint Directorate of Military Support
JFLCC	Joint Forces Land Component Command
JOA	Joint Operations Area
JTF	Joint Task Force
JTF-CS	Joint Task Force Civil Support
NG	National Guard
NGB	National Guard Bureau
NORAD	North American Aerospace Defense Command
NPS	National Planning Scenarios
PCA	Posse Commitatus Act
PTDO	Prepare to Deploy Order
QDR	Quadrennial Review
RAND	Research and Development Corporation
SECDEF	Secretary of Defense
TTP	Tactics, Techniques and Procedures
ULO	Unified Land Operation
USNORTHCOM	United States Northern Command
USC	United States Code

U.S. PACOM	United States Pacific Command
U.S. TRANSCOM	United States Transportation Command
WAS	Wide Area Security
WMD	Weapons of Mass Destruction

TABLES

INTRODUCTION

The terrorist threat to the United States today remains complex. While not every chemical, biological, radiological, or nuclear (CBRN) threat is from terrorists, or even manmade, preparation for terrorist attacks predominates because of the increasing threat from terrorist groups armed with weapons of mass destruction.[1] Although the military decreased portions of the threat over the past ten years by implementing changes to the military organization in support to the homeland, the threat remains relevant. Should the worst happen, such as an attack with a weapon of mass destruction or a CBRN incident, federal and state National Guard forces would provide specialized capabilities and general-purpose forces.[2] While major strides in planning, preparation, funding, and training in support of homeland defense and civil support occurred, lack of interagency coordination and execution among all stakeholders remains a challenge. Before September 11, 2001, the Department of Defense failed to assign command authority of military forces in support to civil authorities to any combatant commander. In the wake of 9/11, the Secretary of Defense assigned to USNORTHCOM the mission of providing military forces in support of civilian authorities in case of a natural disaster or a terrorist attack anywhere in the U.S. or its territories.

With this directive, USNORTHCOM planners formed Joint Task Force Civil Support (JTF-CS) with the mission of providing assistance to civilian authorities when requested by state governors and approved by the President of the United States. To fulfill mission requirements this Joint Task Force contains multiple units across the United States in support of a myriad of potential scenarios. In the structure of JTF-CS, there are representatives from the Army, Air Force, and Navy prepared to deploy within 24-48 hours' notice to assist civilian authorities based

---

[1]Department of the Army, *Army Doctrine Publication 3-28 Defense Support to Civil Authorities,* (Washington D.C.: Government Printing Office, August 2012), 11.

[2]Ibid., 11.

1

on identified gaps in state capabilities. The complexity of bringing together all capabilities at the local, state, federal and non-governmental organizations coherently at the appropriate time is as daunting as the importance of the mission.

Distributed across the USNORTHCOM area of responsibility, these military forces must follow a strict deployment timeline set by USNORTHCOM. The majority of Defense Support of Civil Authorities (DSCA) missions will stress the sustainment warfighting function. Mission success depends on units' ability to deliver personnel, medical support, supplies, and equipment, while maintaining their equipment and soldiers. This is challenging because forces often provide support in areas devastated by a disaster and lacking potable water, electrical power, and sanitation. When needed, a federal installation identified as a base support installation will serve as a base for federal military forces throughout the mission.[3] In order to support deployment of military forces, base support installations should synchronize and coordinate deployment support efforts to ensure military forces abide to USNORTHCOM timelines. Factors that this research will consider are the location of deploying military forces in relation to the incident area, capabilities, and requirements necessary to transport military forces to support civilian authorities. Successful synchronization will safeguard a unified effort among all stakeholders to include military forces and civilian authorities.

As USNORTHCOM completes its first decade of existence the hard question arises: Does USNORTHCOM have the capacity to deliver support to civil authorities in response to natural disasters and CBRNE attacks in a matter consistent with the reasonable expectations of the American people? Many aspects are at stake that would require analysis such as the basis to determine if forces available to USNORTHCOM are sufficient or if military forces can rapidly deploy and arrive within 72 hours to support civil authorities.

---

[3]Ibid., 4.

DOD identified capability gaps in its civil support mission by completing a capabilities-based assessment in March 2010. The overarching recommendation is that key DOD policies and guidance for the civil support mission are outdated, limiting DOD's ability to fully address capability gaps. DOD's strategic guidance requires that military forces in conjunction with civil authorities anticipate requests for civil support by identifying capability gaps based on up-to-date guidance.[4] However, inconsistency and misalignment across DOD's policies, strategy, and doctrine for civil support makes interagency coordination difficult for DOD to address capability gaps and pre-position equipment and supplies. A Government Accountability Office (GAO) report published in March 2010, found outdated DOD policies and guidance that do not reflect current organizational framework for providing assistance to civil authorities. A solution suggested by the GAO is that if DOD updates key policies for civil support, it will be better able to address capability gaps and provide timely and appropriate support to civil authorities.[5] A current example is DOD's recent publication, Army Doctrine Publication 3-0, *Unified Land Operations* (ADP 3-0). Notwithstanding addressing defense support of civil authorities, ADP 3-0 lacks the necessary details that allow military forces to plan appropriately.

This monograph makes two fundamental assumptions. First, the United States will remain militarily engaged in the world to ensure that the national interests are protected. As a result, its national security strategy of "Security, Prosperity, Values, and International Order"[6] and its national military strategy of "Prevent, Shape, and Win" will remain unchanged in

---

[4]U.S. Government Accountability Office, *DoD Can Enhance Efforts to Identify Capabilities to Support Civil Authorities during Disasters,* (Washington, DC: U.S. Government Accountability Office, June 2008), 3.

[5]Ibid., 16.

[6]The White House, *National Security Strategy*, (Washington D.C.: Government Printing Office, May 2010), 11.

principle, even if the terms and priorities change.[7] Second, if U.S. national culture and historical

traditions are any indication, American citizens will demand a domestic environment in which

their homeland is secure, but the primacy of civilian authority and liberties remain intact and

security measures are transparent.[8] Once states have exhausted their ability to deal with an

emergency and their internal capabilities are exhausted then the federal government will provide

the support requested. In essence, the U.S. military will perform the bulk of its Homeland

Security missions as the supporting rather than the lead federal agency and may have to comply

with restrictive rules established by civilian authorities.[9]

---

[7]Chairman, Joint Chiefs of Staff, *The National Military Strategy of the United States*, (Washington, D.C., February 8, 2011), 5.

[8]In a speech to the National Academy of Sciences on January 22, 1998, President Bill Clinton assured the public that those demands would be met, declaring that even in the face of a growing bioterrorist threat, the government would remain committed to upholding "privacy rights and other constitutional protections, as well as the proprietary rights of American businesses."

[9]Thomas R. Lujan, "Legal Aspects of Domestic Employment of the Army," *Parameters*, Vol. 27, No. 3, Autumn 1997, 82-97.

HISTORIC CONTEXT OF DEFENSE SUPPORT OF CIVIL AUTHORITIES (DSCA)

Prior to September 11, 2001, domestic military missions frequently lacked adequate coordination among the uniformed services, were ad hoc and poorly resourced, and were generally executed in a manner inconsistent with the "jointness" required by the 1986 Goldwater–Nichols Act. The Secretary of Defense recognized that this approach was inadequate to address the foreseeable and substantial threats likely to emerge in a post–9/11 environment. In the case of DSCA, missions have been authorized and defined by a diverse array of specific statutes and directives.[10] The federal government has rarely considered natural and non-terror-human caused disasters within the United States to be matters of national security that required intervention of military forces. The notable exception was civil defense in case of a nuclear attack. The air defenses assigned to North American Aerospace Defense Command (NORAD) were the main protection against an air attack to the U.S. homeland. The maritime approaches were under the de facto authority of the Chief of Naval Operations. Land-based military capabilities were oriented toward very specific mission sets: force protection, counter-narcotics, civil disturbance, and, when requested by a governor and approved by the president, civil support.[11] While substantial capability to defend against chemical, biological, radiological, nuclear, and high explosive (CBRNE) weapons existed within the Department of Defense (DOD), the assets specifically identified for domestic employment were principally allocated to joint Task Force Civil Support (JTF-CS).

---

[10]Patrick A. Barnett, "Domestic Operational Law Handbook for Judge Advocates" U.S. Department of Defense, Directive 3025.18, December 29, 2010, http://www.dtic.mil/whs/directives/corres/pdf/302518p.pdf (accessed January 2013).

[11]"Defense Support of Civil Authorities (DSCA) Handbook", *Tactical Level Commander and Staff Toolkit 2011*, http://www.survivalebooks.com (accessed November 2012), 3.

In April 2002, the DOD created a new geographic combatant command: Northern Command (U.S.NORTHCOM).[12] Its geographic area of responsibility consisted of the 48 continental U.S. states, Alaska, the District of Columbia, Puerto Rico, the U.S. Virgin Islands, Canada and Mexico. Of note, DOD delegated the same set of responsibilities to U.S. Pacific Command in order to provide assistance to U.S. areas outside USNORTHCOM's area of responsibilities such as Hawai'i, Guam, Northern Mariana Islands, and American Samoa. USNORTHCOM's assigned responsibilities fall into two broad categories:

1. Homeland Defense–the protection of U.S. sovereignty, territory, domestic population, and critical defense infrastructure against external threats as directed by the president.[13]

2. Defense Support of Civil Authorities–is DOD support, including federal military forces, the department's career civilian and contractor personnel, and DOD agency and components assets, for domestic emergencies and for designated law enforcement and other activities.[14]

The defense community, including USNORTHCOM, also continued to evolve and grow into this new mission. In 2002, the Secretary of Defense recommended, and Congress approved, a new command position–the Assistant Secretary of Defense for Homeland Defense and Americas Security Affairs. Congress also approved the elevation of the Joint Directorate of Military Support (JDOMS), which approves requests for military support to civilian authorities, moving it to the Operations Directorate of the Joint Staff.[15]

---

[12]Ibid., 8.

[13]Department of Defense, *Quadrennial Defense Review Report*, (Washington, D.C., February 2010), 10-1.

[14]Ibid., 7.

[15]Donald F. Thompson, "Terrorism and Domestic Response: Can DOD Help Get it

INITIAL DOD EFFORTS TO BUILD A STATE LEVEL MILITARY RESPONSE

Background

USNORTHCOM's initial concept of operations anticipated the necessary operating forces, including critical lifesaving capabilities, would be under its command structure only in the aftermath of a major disaster when directed by the President of the United States. Until then, such allocated forces would remain with their parent services conducting normal day-to-day operations at their respective installations across the United States. By design, this concept of operations lacks the direct attention that leaders, planners, and interagency liaison offices needed to provide the operational capability within moments notice.

The historic view and core principle of American history is that the federal military should play a very limited role within U.S. borders. Federalist No. 8[16] significantly influenced this decision not to assign forces to USNORTHCOM. Another factor also came into play: an institutional aversion by the Department of Defense to the entire DSCA mission set. Many senior DOD leaders–civilian and uniformed alike–believed that providing support to civil authorities was a mission of secondary importance. DSCA mission set was important but only if military forces could be spared from more important combat missions in Iraq and Afghanistan. The emerging DSCA missions in the USNORTHCOM portfolio–National Planning Scenarios–did not fit the DOD's warrior ethos model. Army forces provide the majority of military support during a domestic catastrophe, mainly through the National Guard (NG). State National Guard forces include Army and Air National Guard serving under active duty status or Title 32.[17] In 2008 the

---

Right?" *Joint Force Quarterly* 40, 1st Quarter 2006, 17, http://www.ndu.edu/inss/Press/jfq_pages/edition/i40/i40.pdf (Accessed September 2012).

[16]Alexander Hamilton, The Library of Congress, "Federalist Papers," Federalist 8, http://thomas.loc.gov/home/histdox/fedpapers.html (accessed January 2013).

[17]Department of the Army, *Army Doctrine Publication 3-28 Defense Support to Civil*

Commission on the National Guard and Reserves report *Transforming the National Guard and Reserves into a 21st Century Operational Force*, rightly emphasized the need to overcome DOD's cultural resistance to domestic civil support missions.[18] Based on this cultural resistance the Commission on the National Guard and Reserves called for congressional action to expressly clarify DOD's duty to provide civil support. The commission further noted that Congress should:

1. Codify "the Department of Defense's current responsibility, as defined in its Strategy for Homeland Defense and Civil Support. In other words, the law should state that DOD has the responsibility to provide support to the Department of Homeland Security (DHS) and other agencies for domestic emergencies and for designated law enforcement and other activities."[19]

2. Declare that, "responding to natural and man-made disasters in the homeland is a core competency of DOD that is equal to its combat responsibilities."

3. Clearly state "that in the event of a major catastrophe incapacitating civilian government over a wide geographic area, DOD is expected to provide the bulk of the response".[20]

Over time, National Guard Bureau initiatives produced an integrated and effective system of response for mid-range CBRNE consequence management missions. Following a localized disaster, the governor of the affected state could rapidly deploy NG CBRNE response personnel to assess the incident, determine the CBRNE contaminants, advise first responders, and inform

---

Authorities, (Washington D.C.: Government Printing Office, August 2012), 8.

[18]Jan B. Harkin, ed., "Transforming the National Guard and Reserves Into a 21st Century Operational Force," (Hauppauge, N.Y.: Nova Science Pub Inc, 2010), 19.

[19]Ibid., 23.

[20]Department of the Army, *Army Doctrine Publication 3-28 Defense Support to Civil Authorities,* (Washington D.C.: Government Printing Office, August 2012), 12.

follow-on forces. These units–CBRNE Support Teams (CST), CBRNE Enhanced Response Force Package (CERFP), and Homeland Response Force (HRF)–could also provide their own decontamination and immediate medical care. However, state level entities could not structure their capabilities to respond to the much greater demands of a complex non-contiguous multistate catastrophe because of the amount of limited resources within the state. A multistate catastrophe became an unfamiliar problem to the Department of Homeland Defense and Department of Defense. This unfamiliarity resulted in the creation of Joint Task Force Civil Support (JTF-CS) at the federal level. Army National Guard units have advantages and disadvantages for employment in a domestic role. Significant advantages are proximity, responsiveness, knowledge of local conditions, and closer association with state and local officials. The essential disadvantages for using National Guard forces are wide distribution and capabilities of units between states and limited ability of the states to fund activated National Guard units for extended periods.[21]

WMD Civil Support Teams (CST)

The Army National Guard's consistent emphasis on the need to defend the U.S. homeland against asymmetric catastrophes was the driving force to create the Weapons of Mass Destruction (WMD) Civil Support Teams. The National Guard Bureau leadership saw homeland defense as an integrated element of 21-century national security.[22] This effort to create WMD support teams created a tiered system of capabilities for CBRNE response. As a result, the National Guard working closely with congressional allies, sought and received authorization to

[21]Department of the Army, *Army Doctrine Publication 3-28 Defense Support to Civil Authorities,* (Washington D.C.: Government Printing Office, August 2012), 8.

[22]Department of Defense, *Quadrennial Defense Review Report*, (Washington, D.C., February 2010), 13.

establish 10 CSTs in 1999.[23] A CST is essentially a CBRNE reconnaissance team with the capability to identify CBRNE agents, assess the current and projected consequences of suspected or actual WMD events, advise civilian responders, and assist with request for assistance to expedite arrival of additional state and military assets to help save lives, prevent human suffering, and mitigate property damage.[24]

Congress mandated that each state and territory of the U.S. have at least one CST providing support for immediate response within the state or in support of a territory. By 2000, congress authorized 17 additional CSTs, five more in 2001, and 23 more in 2005 for a total of 55 CSTs therefore covering all states and territories. Two more were approved in 2012, one in New York and one in Florida. CSTs are federally funded NG units established under Presidential Decision Directive 39. There are 57 fulltime teams: one in every U.S. state, Washington, D.C., Puerto Rico, Guam and the US Virgin Islands, and an additional team each in California, Florida and New York.[25] Multiple events that occurred in 2005 such as Hurricane Katrina, Hurricane Rita and Hurricane Wilma began to alert the Secretary of Defense that DOD and the entire federal interagency were not adequately prepared for a domestic catastrophic event, including a WMD attack.

---

[23]Robert J Heyer, "Introduction to CBRNE Terrorism: An Awareness Primer and Preparedness Guide for Emergency Responders", Monograph Series, (Longmont, CO: Disaster Preparedness and Emergency Response Association, 2006), 7.

[24]"Defense Support of Civil Authorities (DSCA) Handbook", Tactical Level Commander and Staff Toolkit 2011, http://www.survivalebooks.com (accessed November 2012), 8.

[25]"Weapons of Mass Destruction – Civil Support Teams", Domestic Preparedness Journal (May 2012), http://c21.maxwell.af.mil/wmd-cst.htm (accessed September 2012).

CBRNE Enhanced Response Forces Packages (CERFP)

Building on the CST concept in 2004, the Chief of the National Guard Bureau proposed

the creation of 17 CERFPs to augment the capabilities within various states. The mission of a

CERFP is to "respond to a CBRNE incident and assist local, state, and federal agencies in

conducting consequence management by providing capabilities to conduct personnel

decontamination, emergency medical services, and casualty search and extraction."[26]

The CERFP NG personnel structure contains a Medical Team (45 personnel), a Search

and Extraction Team (50 personnel), and a Decontamination Team (75 personnel). Each CERFP

has approximately 170-200 personnel trained in catastrophe management drawn from existing

units, normally in state status, but available for Title 32 or, under extraordinary circumstances,

---

[26]Christian M. Van Alstyne, *Potential Standards and Methods for the National Guard's Homeland Response Force,* (Monterey, California: February, 2012), 46.

Title 10 employment.[27] Even though these teams provided a superb capability, CERFPs were limited in numbers and capability to rapidly respond throughout the entire nation. Moreover, in most circumstances, these National Guard units would be under the governor's command and control and therefore would be unavailable to the president during the events of national significance based on the provisions of the Public Law 109-364, the "John Warner Defense Authorization Act of 2007"[28]. For complex, multistate catastrophes, the president would be limited to call on USNORTHCOM. Seventeen states have CERFP teams: California, Colorado, Florida, Georgia, Hawai'i, Illinois, Massachusetts, Minnesota, Missouri, Nebraska, New York, Ohio, Pennsylvania, Texas, Virginia, Washington, and West Virginia. The CERFP teams are strategically based to allow for an expeditious response with at least one CERFP team in each of the 10 Federal Emergency Management Agency regions (Figure 3). Three CERFP teams are in Region 3 (PA, WV, VA) and three more in Region 5 (IL, OH, MN) providing coverage for high population areas in the North/North-East and National Capital Region. Two CERFP teams are in Region 9 (HI, CA) based on population density and geographic location. Two CERFP teams are in Region 4 (GA, FL) and two more in Region 7 (NE, MO) providing capabilities to leverage in the event of a catastrophe on the scale of Hurricane Katrina.[29] In addition to quick activation from the supported governor, CERFP Team distribution within each of the FEMA regions' role is deployment response time and their ability to arrive to a catastrophe. Moreover, there is an increased exposure to training exercises within the CERFP region allowing interoperability with

_____

[27]Ibid., 38.

[28]Bill of Rights Defense Committee (BORDC), Public Law 109-364, the "John Warner Defense Authorization Act of 2007," (H.R.5122) http://www.bordc.org/threats/hr5122.php (accessed January 2013).

[29]Army National Guard, *National Guard CERFP Teams,* http://www.arng.army.mil/News/publications/fs/2010/Subject_papers/ National% 20Guard%20 CERFP%20Teams.pdf (accessed January 2013).

WMD CSTs. The alignments shown in Figure 3, depicts how CERFPs are distributed throughout FEMA regions depicted in roman numerals (Figure 3).

The alignment between CERFP and FEMA allows for a developed relationship such as training together, understanding the capabilities and limitations of military forces within the region being supported. The CERFP has been successful in responding to medium size disasters under their current structure such as the 2008 flooding in Martinsville, Ind. and Hurricane Katrina in 2005. Nonetheless, a CERFP is limited in scale to the type of catastrophes it can support based on resources and capabilities available within its organization. This lack of scale offers an opportunity to apportion other Title 32 military forces to align regionally with FEMA and augment CERFPs.

The cumulative effect of de-synchronization at the local and state level increases compatibility problems once federal military forces arrive to assist. According to Government Accountability Office Report 12-114, published in December 2011, the National Guard Bureau has a framework in place for the operational command and control of CERFPs that outlines how the teams will integrate with civilian and military command structures. However, the command and control of operations involving CERFPs may be limited because of (1) inadequate communications equipment; (2) the absence of required agreements between some CERFPs and their out-of-state elements which require congressional approval; and (3) infrequent opportunities to practice potential command and control arrangements in a realistic response environment.[30]

Upon notification of a validated pre-positioned or response support request, the NG CERFP Commander will determine the personnel/equipment to be deployed in the response. Commanders will conduct a rapid mission analysis to tailor deployment preparation, manage the alert/recall of NG CERFP units, deployment times and distances, and individual rest plans to facilitate safe deployment and mission readiness. NG CERFPs are capable of self-deployment by ground transportation. Fielded NG CERFP equipment sets and assigned vehicles are also air-transportable by C-130 or larger aircraft. Subsets of NG CERFP mission equipment are man-portable for rotary wing movement, however, use of subsets reduce overall mission execution, triage, decontamination, and medical treatment throughput capabilities. Within a 500 mile transportation radius of the NG CERFP, an assumption can be made that airlift for movement will not be used when it would not substantially reduce travel time to the incident location.

---

[30]U.S. Government Accountability Office, *Homeland Defense And Weapons Of Mass Destruction Additional Steps Could Enhance the Effectiveness of the National Guard's Life-Saving Response Forces,* (Washington, DC: U.S. Government Accountability Office, December 2011), 2.

Transport Means	less than 150 miles	150 - 250 miles	greater than 250 miles
Self-Deploy (Vehicles)	3 hrs or less	3 hrs to 5 hrs	5 hrs plus
Rotary Wing Aircraft	3.5 hrs	3.5 hrs to 4.5 hrs	4.5 hrs plus
Fixed Wing Aircraft	4.75 hrs after positioning aircraft and crew	4.75 hrs to 5.25 hrs after positioning aircraft and crew	5.25 hrs plus after positioning aircraft and crew

Table 1 CERFP Movements – National Response Planning Timelines

Source: http://www.ngbpdc.ngb.army.mil/pubs/10/ngr500-4_angi10-2504.pdf

To facilitate integration into the disaster support efforts the NG CERFP Commander is in a position to provide valuable civil military coordination information to other military response elements. NG CERFPs will task organize in accordance with their capabilities and the JTF Commander's mission and intent. Requests for information from military agencies outside the NG CERFP chain of command will be directed to the JTF at the state level or the NGB Joint Operations Center. NG CERFPs are national assets that serve a critical role in the homeland defense mission. Simultaneously, NG CERFPs provide a response capability for their respective state, territory, or the District of Columbia or as otherwise governed by state-to-state agreements.

<u>Homeland Response Force (HRF)</u>

Based on the 2010 Quadrennial Defense Review and Office of the Secretary of Defense (OSD) decisions, ten new 566-person domestic chemical biological radiological nuclear and explosive (CBRNE) and all-hazards response organizations were created to meet regional response requirements.[31] Envisioning scenarios in which extremely large scale

---

[31]Department of Defense, *Quadrennial Defense Review Report*, (Washington, D.C., February 2010), 14.

incidents might require the activation of CSTs and/or CERFPs from multiple states, the Secretary of Defense directed the National Guard Bureau to design yet another new kind of task force model –one that would be optimized to provide command and control (C2) of these CBRNE– from multiple states. This new type of brigade level C2 element is called a Homeland Response Force. In addition to its Headquarters element (HQ), each HRF will include a security element and a battalion sized CBRNE task force with the same capabilities as a CERFP. Each HRF is capable of providing command and control for up to five CSTs and three CERFPs and will focus on planning, training, and exercising within its FEMA region, with the goal of establishing links between the local, state, and federal authorities.

To be able to provide broad geographic coverage (and to best align with the federal model), the DOD directed that ten of these Response Forces be established, one per FEMA region. Within each region, one state's National Guard would serve as the host for the Response Force. Like the CERFP, the Homeland Response Force would not be a new unit structure increasing the overall size of the host state's forces. Rather, it is a task force designation, requiring the host state to identify existing forces to take on the Response Force mission in addition to its existing missions. These ten teams will be operational over the course of FY 2012 through FY 2013. Even though there are three layers of response (CST, CERFP and, HRF) at the state level, there is still a need for coordination. The lack of coordination when synchronizing the bulk of the capabilities becomes priority in providing support within twenty-four hours at the local and state level. This desynchronization adds complexity when Title 10 federal forces arrive to an incident area to provide additional support once the catastrophe becomes "federalized" at the request of the governor. For this reason the HRF serves as the bridge between Title 32 and Title 10 forces.

For a catastrophe managed at the state level, local response military forces have the bulk of the CBRNE response capability located within the affected state's borders or adjacent states. These state response capabilities deploy to an incident area via organic transportation eliminating dependency from external sources such as U.S. Transportation Command (U.S. TRANSCOM). Although air movement might be needed, most of the time it is not the primary method of transportation due to proximity of assets within the state. Therefore, strict timelines are realistic based on a pre-determined area of responsibility.

The opposite is true at the federal level where (1) USNORTHCOM geographical response area is the United States and territories. Therefore, (2) location of impact area is an unrealistic planning assumption during training exercises when speed of deployment is essential.

(3) DCRF dependency from multiple agencies to transport its military forces adds an additional layer of bureaucracy delaying response. (4) Spread of DCRF organic forces across the United States increases delays in assembling Task Forces to create unity of effort and speed of support to civil authorities.

Because an HRF is expected to bring a wide range of capabilities to an incident scene, they need to be outfitted with a system capable of supporting a diverse set of operations. One key element of this system is command and control of all forces operating in support of the consequence management efforts to include the WMD CSTs and CERFPs.[32] When forming their Joint Operations Area (JOA), each HRF must ask the CST and CERFP operating in the JOA if it has the following capabilities:

1. Rapid Deploy: If HRFs are going to meet their short response posture, they must have facilities that can be set up quickly and easily. The ideal facility should not only feature a quick-erect design, but also require limited loose parts and tools to further reduce deployment time. Additionally, the JOA should require minimal personnel to assist in set up, allowing the majority of forces to focus on actual response efforts.

2. Easily Transportable: Because they must be transportable via ground, HRFs can be easily and quickly transported from one location to the next. In addition to meeting military requirements for ground transport, the equipment must also meet requirements for air transport in the event that an HRF must be moved via aircraft to the incident site.

3. Flexible Organizational Design: A JOA must have the proper space to support the wide range of HRF capabilities, from command and control to decontamination to search and extraction. The operations area must also be able to support the various support equipment that will be needed for each of these capabilities, such as communications gear, medical equipment

---

[32]Homeland Response Force, "Fact Sheet," http://www.defense.gov/news/d20100603hrf.pdf (accessed December 2012).

and water heating systems.

4. Command and Control Ready: Finally, an effective JOA must feature command and control equipment that will allow personnel to receive data from various locations across the incident scene to make informed decisions and properly execute response efforts.[33]

The U.S. Military must establish robust, fully capable response forces unlike any seen before to be prepared for the numerous dangers threatening our current homeland security. From command and control to decontamination to search and extraction, HRFs must be prepared to complete a wide range of operations whenever and wherever disaster strikes.[34] The implementation of Homeland Response Forces during Hurricane Katrina marked a significant change in the way military forces will assist in future response efforts, providing civilian agencies with a more streamlined force that is better equipped to quickly arrive at the incident scene and bring much needed capabilities and technical expertise to the incident scene.

---

[33]Ibid.

[34]U.S. Government Accountability Office, *Homeland Defense And Weapons Of Mass Destruction Additional Steps Could Enhance the Effectiveness of the National Guard's Life-Saving Response Forces,* (Washington, D.C.: U.S. Government Accountability Office, December 2011), 2.

EFFORTS TO BUILD A MULTI-STATE CATASTROPHE MILITARY RESPONSE

The defense of the United States and its territories is the government and DOD's top priority.[35] The range of military operations in the homeland consists of Homeland Defense (HD) and DSCA. The Army defends the homeland and provides support to civil authorities, which are top priorities identified in Guidance for Employment of the Force and National Military Strategy. The HD and DSCA are on the list of ten "Primary Missions of the Armed Forces" as outlined in the new Strategic Guidance for DOD, signed by the president in January 2010.[36] One of the biggest mistakes that tactical commanders can make is to assume they need to take charge upon arrival at the scene of an incident. Military forces operating freely within civilian jurisdiction risk upsetting the constitutional balance between civil authority, the military, and the private sector.[37]

The homeland is a unique and challenging operational environment for the Army and has a special set of requirements that future leaders must understand. The inherent characteristic of being in support of civilian authorities creates friction. By nature, military forces are created to be given a mission, apply capabilities and resources, and fulfill the requirements that will allow the achievement of the political end state.

DSCA is part of the Decisive Action construct that is found in Army doctrine (along with Offense, Defense and Stability Operations), but most Army forces do not have the capabilities needed for HD or DSCA operations in the homeland (some technical support forces are

---

[35]Department of Defense, *National Defense Strategy,* (Washington, D.C.: June 2011), 17-8.

[36]Department of Defense, *Quadrennial Defense Review Report*, (Washington, D.C., February 2010), 10-11.

[37]Department of the Army, *Army Doctrine Publication 3-28 Defense Support to Civil Authorities,* (Washington D.C.: Government Printing Office, August 2012), 6.

required).[38] The employment of military forces to conduct operations within the homeland is constrained by both law and policy. For example, employment of military forces for law enforcement is fundamentally different depending if the military force supporting civilian authorities is activated under Title 10 or Title 32. Commanders are bound by law, under the Posse Comitatus Act, in the employment of Title 10 forces for law enforcement missions therefore, commanders must understand this unique environment before a catastrophe occurs in order to shape activities before and during execution. Unified action is essential when the military responds to our nation's needs. The Army National Guard plays a predominant and unique role in DSCA operations, whether under the mission command of the state governor or federalized as Title 10 under the mission command of the President of the United States, Secretary of Defense, and supported combatant commander. Unity of effort between the state-led and federal-led responses is required for conducting military operations in the homeland.[39]

Regarding the National Guard, the term "activated" simply means that a unit or individual of the reserve components has been called to active duty as prescribed on the written document received. The purpose and authority for that activation will determine limitations and duration of the activation. The Army and Air National Guard may be activated in a number of ways as prescribed by public law. Broadly, there are two titles in the United State Code (USC) under which units and troops may be activated, Title 32 (Militia Code) and Title 10.[40]

---

[38]Department of the Army, *Army Doctrine Publication 3-0 Unified Land Operations,* (Washington D.C.: Government Printing Office, October 2011), 3.

[39]Department of the Army, *Army Posture Statement (APS), "Defense CBRNE Response Force (DCRF),"* information paper, July 2011, https://secureweb2.hqda.pentagon.mil/VDAS_ArmyPostureStatement/2011/information_papers/PostedDocument.asp?id=258 (accessed November 2012).

[40]Army National Guard, National Guard "Fact Sheet," http://www.arng.army.mil/SiteCollectionDocuments/Publications/News%20Media%20Factsheets/ARNG_Factsheet_May_06%20ARNG%20fact%20Sheet.pdf (accessed January 2013).

State Duty

When National Guard units are not under federal control, the governor is the commander-in-chief of the units of his or her respective state, territory (Guam, Virgin Islands), or commonwealth (Puerto Rico). The President of the United States commands the District of Columbia (DC) National Guard, though this command is routinely delegated to the Commanding General of the DC National Guard.[41] States are free to employ their National Guard forces under state control for state purposes and at state expense as provided in the state's constitution and statutes. In doing so, governors, as commanders-in-chief, can directly access and utilize the National Guard's federally assigned aircraft, vehicles, and other equipment so long as the federal government is reimbursed for the use of fungible equipment and supplies such as fuel, and food stocks. This is the authority under which governors activate and deploy National Guard forces in response to natural disasters and man-made emergencies such as riots and civil unrest, or terrorist attacks.[42]

The governor can activate National Guard personnel to "state active duty" in response to natural or man-made disasters or Homeland Defense missions. State Active Duty is based on State statute and policy as well as state funds; Soldiers and Airmen remain under the command and control of their governor. The federal Posse Commitatus Act (PCA) does not apply therefore state soldiers could be used for law enforcement activities. Restrictions on the use of federal military forces for law enforcement activities impair the ability of JTF commanders to employ combinations of Title 10 and Title 32 military forces within the Task Force. For example, a task force comprised of two infantry battalions, one battalion from Montana NG and the other

---

[41]Ibid.

[42]Spencer W. Robinson, "The Role of the Army National Guard in the 21st Century; Peacekeeping Vs. Homeland Security," The National Guard Association of the United States, http://www.ngaus.org/sites/default/files/pdf/primer%20fin.pdf (accessed January 2013).

battalion from the 82nd Infantry Division (Airborne). The JTF commander could not use all forces for law enforcement activities regardless of the battalion command relationship during the civil support operations. Posse Commitatus will take effect and the battalion from Montana NG is the only military force available to the JTF commander to conduct law enforcement activities.

Federal Duty

Title 10 service means full-time duty in the active military service of the United States. The term used is federalized. Federalized National Guard forces have been ordered by the President to active duty either in their reserve component status or by calling them into Federal service in their militia status.[43] There are several forms of activation: voluntary order to active duty, which is with the consent of a soldier or airman and the approval of their governor. Partial Mobilization is another example in time of national emergency declared by the President for any unit or any member for no more than 24 consecutive months.

The unit charged to represent USNORTHCOM and to assist civil authorities in conducting CBRNE CM within the area of responsibility is Joint Task Force Civil Support (JTF-CS). JTF-CS is a standing Joint Task Force headquarters located at Fort Eustis, Virginia. The establishment of this JTF traces back to 1998. JTF-CS stands ready to provide command and control of military resources when called upon to support federal, state and local authorities in the United States, its territories and its possessions as a result of a CBRNE attack or incident within America's borders.

---

[43] Army National Guard, National Guard Fact Sheet, http://www.arng.army.mil/SiteCollectionDocuments/Publications/News%20Media%20Factsheets/ARNG_Factsheet_May_06%20ARNG%20fact%20Sheet.pdf (accessed January 2013).

National Planning Scenarios (NPS)

The Federal interagency community has developed fifteen all-hazards planning scenarios (the National Planning Scenarios) for use in national, federal, state, and local homeland security preparedness activities in order to establish a reference and provide the basis to train the most likely scenarios. The national planning scenarios serve as planning tools and are representative of the range of potential terrorist attacks and natural disasters. The objective was to develop a minimum number of credible scenarios in order to establish the range of response requirements to facilitate preparedness planning.[44] Some of the national planning scenarios are: nuclear detonation, biological attack, biological disease outbreak (pandemic influenza), chemical attack of various types, natural disasters, radiological attacks, and cyber attack.[45]

Since these scenarios were compiled to be the minimum number necessary to develop the range of response capabilities and resources, other hazards were inevitably omitted. Examples of other potentially high-impact events include nuclear power plant incidents, industrial and transportation accidents, and natural disasters however, leaving uncovered the full range of potential dangerous scenarios. Entities at all levels of government can use the National Planning Scenarios as a reference to help them identify the scope, magnitude, and complexity of potential major events. Civilian agencies and military forces can also develop their own scenarios to supplement the National Planning Scenarios.[46]

The principal responsibility for the prevention of and protection from acts of terror is at the federal level. Consequently, the fifteen NPS focus on acts of terror and major natural

---

[44]Department of Homeland Security, National Preparedness Guidelines, http://www.dhs.gov/national-preparedness-guidelines (accessed December 2012).

[45]Ibid.

[46]Ibid.

disasters, such as hurricanes and earthquakes. In the early stages of developing homeland security national preparedness public policy, DHS, in cooperation with state, tribal, territorial, and local governments, identified capabilities-based planning (CBP) as the planning system to be used in building preparedness across the nation. Since threats to the United States are not static, preparedness requires the ability to adapt and respond in the face of uncertainty. CBP helps account for this uncertainty by ensuring that planning is not limited to addressing the specific aspects of certain threats, but rather focuses on capabilities needed on a range of known and unknown threats.[47]

Each of the National Planning Scenarios represents a highly destructive event. These events captured on the scenarios include terrorist attacks, natural disasters, and technological emergencies. Even though the full scope of these disasters rarely occurs, the conception of their magnitude from experiences during exercises should give military forces a reason to assess their ability to support civil authorities within 48 hours of notification.

The current NPS have been useful for planning and describing the homeland security capabilities and identifying mission partners. The NPS created a common vocabulary and provided a set of scenarios to state and federal agencies to uncover planning disconnects between partners and analyze homeland security risk. The availability of a scenario set produced with federal interagency participation and vetting has introduced some consistency in U.S. government homeland security planning. Although it is essential to note that there is no plan in DHS to update the NPS or to ensure that there is military integration in the integrated planning system.[48]

---

[47]Mary T. Tyszkiewicz, *Journal of Homeland Security and Emergency Management*, Volume 9, Issue 1 Article 32, http://www.journalhsdemer.org/adapt (accessed January 2013).

[48]Ibid.

Current Force Structure: JTF-CS/Defense CBRNE Reaction Force (DCRF)

The CBRNE DCRF is a team of about 5,200 joint personnel who deploy as DOD's initial response force to a CBRNE incident. In terms of Soldiers and combat power, DCRF is approximately an Army division (-) with additional capabilities to support civil authorities commanded by a major general. Using FM 3-35, *Army Deployment and Redeployment,* this monograph will analyze all the necessary steps to ensure military forces can arrive to the site of the catastrophe and support civil authorities as expected by USNORTHCOM and synchronize effectively with local and state forces already operating in the area.

Each DCRF is composed of four functional task forces–Task Force Operations, Task Force Medical, Task Force Logistics and Task Force Aviation–that have their own individual operational focus and set of mission skills. Their capabilities include search and rescue, decontamination, medical, aviation, communications and logistical support. As a partner in the National Response Framework, DOD provides support to state and local authorities managing responses to natural disasters. However, the forces, equipment, and experience required to effectively respond to a CBRNE incident are very different from those needed to respond to natural disasters. The DCRF was established to develop the expertise and maintain the focus on the mission of providing command and control during domestic CBRNE Consequence Management (CM) missions. The CJCS CBRNE Consequence Management Execute Order (EXORD) articulates the authorization and designation of forces.[49] DOD CM support and assistance to civil authorities may require DOD's robust logistical roles, skills, and structures, such as the ability to mobilize large numbers of people, to move large amounts of material and equipment, and to provide other logistical support beyond civil authority capability.

---

[49]United States Army Combined Arms Center, "Joint Task Force-Civil," (information paper), http://usacac.army.mil/cac2/call/docs/10-16/ch_6.asp (accessed November 2012).

On Oct. 1, 2008, US Army North (ARNORTH), as USNORTHCOM's, Joint Force Land Component Commander (JFLCC), assumed operational control of JTF-CS. Furthermore, in representation of the JFLCC, JTF-CS mission is to deploy in response to a weapon of mass destruction attack with CBRNE consequences; a team of military and civilian planners then executes a plan that brings a variety of military capabilities to assist the federal, state and local agencies in response to CBRNE incidents within 48 hours of notification to CBRNE incidents in the homeland.[50]

Deployment Response

Ensuring that military can arrive quickly to support civil authorities upon request of the governor and the president's approval is paramount to save lives, reduce human suffering, and protect property and infrastructure. Deployment is composed of activities required to prepare and move forces, supplies, and equipment to a theater. This includes the force as it task organizes, tailors itself for movement based on the mission, concept of operations, available lift, and other resources.[51] The employment concept of military forces in support to civil authorities is the starting point for deployment planning. Proper planning establishes what, where, and when forces are needed and sets the stage for a successful deployment. Subsequently how the incident commander intends to employ military capabilities available is the basis for orchestrating the deployment structure. *FM 3-35 Deployment and Redeployment* establishes a deployment-goal baseline that stems from the Army Campaign Plan. The plan identifies goals as follow:

- Deploy and employ a brigade combat team (BCT) capability in 4-7 days.

---

[50]Defense Support to Civil Authorities (DSCA) Handbook, Vols. GTA 90-01-20, (Washington, D.C.: U.S. Government Printing Office, 2011).

[51]Department of the Army, *FM 3-35 Deployment and Redeployment,* (Washington D.C.: Government Printing Office, April 2010), 11.

- Deploy and employ three BCTs with a division headquarters in 10 days.

Using *FM 3-35 Deployment and Redeployment* as a starting point to determine the feasibility of deploying JTF-CS is not useful. The support that civilian authorities need within the specified timeline directed by USNORTHCOM in theory position JTF-CS forces on the ground 48 hours from notification. Civilian authorities to coordinate efforts and distribute resources during consequence management operations use these unrealistic timelines based on fictitious exercises that cannot replicate real world conditions. State governments expect federal support to arrive within 48 hours as stipulated in USNORTHCOM CONPLAN 3500.Throughout history there are many examples that show federal military forces inability to meet the 48 hours timeline to provide support from notification.

As recent as Hurricane Sandy, President Barack H. Obama signed an emergency declaration for N.J. 48 hours ahead of the hurricane landfall.[52] On October 26, 2012, President Obama declared Hurricane Sandy as an imminent state of emergency alerting DCO/DCE through USNORTHCOM for potential call up of forces. As per CJCS EXORD declaring a state of emergency should constitute a notification message for DCRF for potential call up–N hour sequence–in response to the strict timeline of 48 hours to deploy specified by the order.[53] Based on actual movement tables of military forces apportioned to JTF-CS from the identified force package one, military forces were arriving at the incident site on Nov 8, 2012.[54]

---

[52]The Associated Press, *Obama signs emergency declaration for N.J. ahead of Hurricane Sandy*, http://www.nj.com/news/index.ssf/2012/10/obama_signs_emergency_declarat.html (accessed January 2013).

[53]N hour sequence designates notification time for military forces to get ready and prepare to deploy.

[54]Federal Emergency Management Agency, "Hurricane Sandy Timeline," http://www.fema.gov/hurricane-sandy-timeline (accessed January 2013).

STATE AND FEDERAL PLANNING INTEGRATION

The National Guard is the logical element of the U.S. armed forces to act as the lead military agency for homeland security. By law and tradition, the National Guard connects local communities to the state and federal government. Units are located among American communities, and they have the capabilities, legal authority, and structure to respond to attacks on the homeland. For example the Army National Guard maintains over 3,000 armories around the nation and the Air National Guard has 140 units throughout the United States and its territories. This close relationship between National Guard units and their locales must be leveraged to ensure that local National Guard units are prepared to respond to attacks.[55]

State relationships with federal forces such as training collaboration and integrated planning are imperative for cross-coordination during a catastrophe. Inequality of roles among states leads to confusion during emergencies. An example of such de-synchronization between state governors and Defense Coordinating Officers (DCO) was captured in July 2010 during an Advisory Panel on Department of Defense Capabilities for Support of Civil Authorities. Dr. James Carafano,[56] one of the nation's leading experts on defense affairs, military operations, strategy, and homeland security, and also a member of the panel noted that USNORTHCOM seems to be moving toward a model of anticipatory response in support of civil authorities as mandated by the QDR 2010. This anticipatory model uses the Defense Coordinating Officer (DCO) as the cornerstone for the model's efficacy. Dr. Carafano believes that the DCO is not the best tool for this job because it lacks the capacity and expertise at its level. He asked for thoughts

---

[55]The Heritage Foundation, "The Role of the National Guard in Homeland Security: Heritage Foundation," http://www.heritage.org/about/staff/departments/douglas-and-sarah-allison-center-for-foreign-policy-studies (accessed December 2012).

[56]James Carafano, Ph.D., Deputy Director, Kathryn and Shelby Cullom Davis Institute for International Studies; Director, Douglas and Sarah Allison Center for Foreign Policy Studies, Heritage Foundation.

from the governors of Vermont and Washington on the anticipatory model and DCO roles. Governor Jim Douglas from Vermont responded that this topic has not been covered in the Council of Governors yet. Governor Christine Gregoire from Washington stated that while she finds the concept very interesting, she has never interacted with a DCO in her six years as governor, and she has overseen a number of disasters within her state.[57]

On September 2010, an independent panel from the U.S. House Armed Services Committee evaluated the 2010 Quadrennial Defense Review and recommended a re-examination of the role of the National Guard with "an eye to ensuring that a portion of the National Guard be dedicated to and funded for homeland defense."[58] Additionally, in September 2010, *National Defense Magazine* published an article describing the House Armed Services Committee findings stating, "our panel thinks we really need to re-think the relationship between the active force and the Guard and reserve, and whether we even need some mobilization capability beyond the Guard and reserve," and take some of the pressure off the active force."[59] The National Guard Bureau's chief, GEN Craig McKinley, states that his major frustration is the difficulty of sharing intelligence with state adjutants general offices because of red tape and firewalls. McKinley stated that he was unable to get information from the Federal Bureau of Investigation (FBI) and Central Intelligence Agency (CIA) to the appropriate National Guard channels. He added that there was a continuing struggle to find ways to break down the barriers of classification and

---

[57]RAND Corporation, "Advisory Panel on Department of Defense Capabilities for Support of Civil Authorities After Certain Incidents," Meeting Minutes, September 2009, http://www.rand.org/content/dam/rand/www/external/nsrd/DOD-CBRNE-Panel/panel/meetings/20100602/20100602-meeting-minutes.pdf (accessed January 2013).

[58]Grace V. Jean, "National Guard Chief: Our Weaknesses Are Here At Home," National Defense Magazine, September 2010, http://www.nationaldefensemagazine.org/archive/2010/September/Pages/OurWeaknessesAreHereAtHome.aspx (accessed November 2012).

[59]Ibid.

31

communication, to push the same information that Defense Department officials have down to those people who can actually use it and maybe prevent another incident such as that of September 11, 2001.[60]

An example of some of the collaboration challenges among agencies responding to disasters was experienced during Hurricane Katrina in 2005. About four days after Hurricane Katrina's landfall the military began providing imagery data from some of its satellites and airplanes dedicated to support civilian agencies, although some information was classified due to its source and could not be shared directly with civilian agencies. Additionally, some agencies were not able to access some of the available information because the data files were too large to download due to an unforecasted bandwidth problem. A National Guard Hurricane Katrina after-action review reported that the adjutants general of Mississippi and Louisiana required real-time imagery that the military community should have been able to provide, but did not. Because state and local officials were overwhelmed and the military's extensive reconnaissance capabilities were not effectively leveraged, responders began organizing and deploying without fully understanding the extent of the damage or the required assistance.[61]

Most of the challenges today between interagency partners were not addressed in the *2010 Quadrennial Review* as the priority for homeland defense. The DOD determined that the priorities needed to be addressed are in fielding faster, more flexible consequence management response forces, enhanced capabilities for domain awareness, accelerate the development of standoff radiological/nuclear detection capabilities and, enhance domestic counter-IED

---

[60]Ibid.

[61]U.S. Government Accountability Office, *Enhanced Leadership, Capabilities, and Accountability Controls Will Improve the Effectiveness of the Nation's Preparedness, Response, and Recovery System,* (Washington, DC: U.S. Government Accountability Office, September 2006), 2.

capabilities.[62] Although the 2010 QDR acknowledges that combatant commanders lack sufficient tools to support their theater campaign plans and their assigned mission to build partner capacity, DOD dismisses the importance of interagency coordination as a mandate to all federal agencies.

Regardless of whether civil support remains a responsibility divided between active duty and National Guard and Reserve forces, it is likely that interagency coordination will be addressed. Extensive coordination will then be necessary to determine what level of investment will be required to meet civil support expectations. Information exchange is a priority and a challenge to overcome in order to increase the speed of deployment in support of civil authorities.

Case Study 1: Hurricane Katrina Response (August 2005)

The issue that has attracted the most attention in post-Katrina discussions has been the speed of rescue and relief operations. The Secretary of Homeland Security, Michael Chertoff, did not declare Hurricane Katrina an Incident of National Significance until August 30, the evening after the hurricane made landfall, making the argument of preemptive federal response capability under the NRP invalid.[63]

USNORTHCOM began its alert and coordination procedures significantly before Katrina's landfall and the subsequent levee breaches. It is not exactly clear when DHS/FEMA first requested DOD assistance or what was specifically requested. Press releases and reports to date, show that DOD made its own assessments of what resources would be useful and began moving towards deployment before or shortly after Katrina's landfall. However, many military

---

[62]Department of Defense, *Quadrennial Defense Review Report*, (Washington, D.C., February 2010), 20.

[63]U.S. Department of Commerce National Oceanic and Atmospheric Administration National Marine Fisheries Service, *Report To Congress On The Impacts Of Hurricanes Katrina, Rita, And Wilma*, http://www.nmfs.noaa.gov/msa2007/docs/Fisheries_Report_Final.pdf (accessed December 2012).

deployments did not begin not until after the presidential declaration of a federal emergency on August 30, and the declaration of an Incident of National Significance on August 31. This procedure although in keeping with the National Response Plan and DOD's Homeland Security Doctrine, may have slowed the arrival of needed DOD assets in the affected region.[64]

Another factor that affected deployments in support of Hurricane Katrina was simply in keeping most relief assets out of the storm's path until it passed in order to avoid their own destruction. However, an earlier and phased deployment could have brought assets closer to the affected region in a more timely fashion. The relief assets' approach was also slowed to some extent by damage to airports/airbases, highways, and the concern about underwater obstructions in the New Orleans Port area. Even after the activation of JTF-Katrina on 30 August, DOD's response appears incremental, as it responded to an increasingly deteriorating situation. The hospital ship *USS Comfort* was not dispatched from Baltimore until 31 August. Additional active duty ground forces (82nd Infantry Division (Airborne), 1st Cavalry Division) did not begin deploying until 3 September, arriving approximately four days after landfall.[65]

Case Study 2: Hurricane Sandy Response (October 2012)

On 27 October 2012, the President of the U.S. declared a national emergency in response to Hurricane Sandy's imminent threat. USNORTHCOM placed DSCA forces on 24-hour Prepare to Deploy Order (PTDO) status on October 29, in response to anticipated FEMA requests to mitigate or respond to effects of Hurricane Sandy.[66] Military in support of civil authorities that are part of JTF-CS require 48 to 96 hours to deploy once placed on a PTDO status. On 26

---

[64]Ibid.

[65]Ibid.

[66]United States Northern Command, *U.S. Northern Command's Support to Hurricane Sandy*, http://www.northcom.mil/News/2012/102912.html, (accessed January 2013).

October 2012 Defense Coordinating Officers deployed to begin coordination with FEMA and to estimate the level of required Title 10 forces support. Based on the FEMA timeline of support, on November 2, DCO continued to estimate the need for additional support. On approximately November 9, USNORTHCOM directed assets arrived with approximately 4000 soldiers to support FEMA.[67]

Joint Task Force Civil Support is an already tailored force ready to support civil authorities upon request. Based on the DSCA EXORD forces are capable to be on the ground to support in approximately 48-96 hours. Forces arrived approximately two weeks following the first broadcasted television news reported that Hurricane Sandy was going to cause damage to the east coast of the U.S. Additionally, the arrival was over a week after the President of the U.S. declared a national emergency. Why was the response slow?

There are studies conducted by RAND Corporation that show there was a lack of understanding by state civil authorities as to DOD's Title 10 role in disaster response, further indicating a need for the building of a collaborative relationship.[68] The first study published in 2006 by RAND surveyed local, state, and health authorities. It indicated that the events of Hurricane Katrina, "...highlighted the differing expectations that state and local officials have with respect to the role of federal military and the National Guard in responding to a major catastrophe."[69] It went on to state that differing expectations of the military could have been in part due to the lack of knowledge of legal restrictions or even misunderstandings about roles and

---

[67]Federal Emergency Management Agency, Hurricane Sandy Timeline, http://www.fema.gov/hurricane-sandy-timeline (accessed January 2013).

[68]Lois M. Davis, Louis T. Mariano, Jennifer E. Pace, Sarah K. Cotton, Paul Steinberg, *Combating Terrorism: How Prepared Are State and Local Response Organizations*, (Santa Monica, CA: RAND Corporation, 2006), p. XVIII, 13.

[69]Ibid., 15.

responsibilities of the military during domestic responses.[70]

ADP 3-0 Unified Land Operations and DSCA

Within Joint Task Force Civil Support military forces organization, the Army is the service that provides the bulk of the forces. Therefore, it is important to understand how Army forces understand defense support of civil authorities (DSCA) within their doctrinal context. In October 2011, the Army unveiled Army Doctrine Publication (ADP) 3-0, Unified Land Operations, the replacement for FM 3-0, Operations. Under the Doctrine 2015 initiative, the new ADPs replace the traditional FMs with concise discussions of general principles of only ten to twelve pages. ADP 3-0 constitutes the Army's view of how it conducts prompt and sustained operations on land and forms the basis for the common operational concept for the Army.

The foundation of Unified Land Operations (ULO) is the Army's warfighting doctrine. It is based on the idea that Army units seize, retain, and exploit the initiative to gain a position of relative advantage. This is accomplished through simultaneous combination of offensive, defensive, and stability operations–ADP 3-0 misses DSCA as part of the foundation of ULO–that set the conditions for favorable conflict resolution.[71] At the center stage of this doctrine is the Decisive Action (DA) construct, which encompass offensive, defensive, stability operations and defense support to civil authorities (Figure 5).

The Army's only two core competencies –combined arms maneuver (CAM) and wide area security (WAS)– provide the means for balancing the application of the warfighting functions within the tactical actions and tasks inherent in the Decisive Action construct which has defense support of civil authorities at its center stage. The debate that emerges from the decisive

[70]Ibid., 39.

[71]Department of the Army, *Army Doctrine Publication 3-0 Unified Land Operations,* (Washington D.C.: Government Printing Office, October 2011), 5.

action construct's discussion, at the School of Advanced Military Studies, is that military forces in support of civil authorities cannot be decisive while employing the core competencies in a support role. Additionally the measures of effectiveness are very difficult to manage when the conditions for favorable conflict resolution falls to another agency such as FEMA when the preponderance of capabilities resides within the military forces.

Based on ADP 3-0, the role of Army forces resides in their capabilities to protect the homeland abroad based on their ability to simultaneously apply CAM and WAS. Even though DSCA is part of the DA construct, ADP 3-0 is not clear in explaining how Army forces will operate in support of civil authorities. This lack of clarity adds complexity to Army forces responding to a call for civilian support when the core of military training is CAM and WAS as explained in the Army's capstone doctrine. When examining Army forces performing operations in an interagency support role, ADP 3-0 misses the mark.

CONCLUSION

A responsibility of any government and its defense establishment is to protect the lives and safety of its people. Because the United States benefits from favorable geography and continental size, direct attacks against the country itself have been rare throughout its history. However, events since the terrorist attacks of September 11, 2001, remind us that the rapid proliferation of destructive technologies, combined with potent ideologies of violent extremism, portends a future in which all governments will have to maintain a high level of vigilance against terrorist threats. Moreover, terrorists are acquiring new means to strike targets at greater distances from their borders and with greater lethality. Finally, the United States must also be prepared to respond to the full range of potential natural disasters.

The experiences of the past several years have deepened the realization that state and non-state adversaries alike may seek to attack military and civilian targets within the United States. Protecting the nation and its people from such threats requires close synchronization between civilian and military efforts. Although many efforts to protect the United States are led by other federal agencies, including the Department of Homeland Security (DHS), the role of the Department of Defense in defending the nation against direct attack and in providing support to civil authorities, potentially in response to a very significant or even catastrophic event, has steadily gained prominence.

To ensure that the Department of Defense is prepared to provide appropriate support to civil authorities, USNORTHCOM must focus JTF-CS and identify capability enhancements that are not available at the local state level. Key initiatives resulting from this monograph include efforts to:

- Field faster, more flexible response forces at the local and state level. The DOD has gained experience and learned valuable lessons from its efforts to field specialized local response teams such as CSTs, CERFPs and HRFs for chemical, biological, radiological, nuclear, and high-yield explosives events. Given the potential for surprise attacks within the United States, the Department must reorganize these forces to enhance their lifesaving capabilities, maximize their flexibility, and reduce their response times. First, DOD should begin restructuring the DCRF, to increase its ability to respond more rapidly to an event at the state level if requested by a governor. This change in force structure should be focused towards counter WMD and early detection. The current force structure seems inadequate to support civil authorities when needed to re-establish normalcy after a catastrophe.

- Complementing the evolution of the DCRF, the DOD also should draw on existing National Guard forces to better train and equip the Homeland Response Forces in each of the ten Federal Emergency Management Agency (FEMA) regions. These ten HRFs will provide a regional response capability; focus on planning, training and exercising; and forge strong links between the federal level and state and local authorities. In lieu of the current fiscal constraints that the Department of Defense is facing, shifting priorities toward an increased state response capability will translate into cost savings.

- Enhance capabilities for situational awareness. USNORTHCOM and its interagency partners must be able to comprehensively monitor the air, land, maritime, space, and cyber domains for potential direct threats to the United States. Such monitoring provides the U.S. homeland with an extended, layered in depth defense. This effort includes enhanced coordination and focus in counter WMD operations. For example, USNORTHCOM working with DHS and the Defense Intelligence Agency (DIA) through a joint technology capability demonstration program to explore new technologies to assists in the identification of gaps in capabilities at the local state level is a potential way to gain better situational awareness.

- Enhance domestic counter WMD capabilities. To better prepare USNORTHCOM to support civil authorities seeking to counter potential threats from domestic WMDs, training must occur that assist civil authorities with tactics, techniques, and procedures

(TTPs) and capabilities developed in recent operations at the local state level.

RECOMMENDATIONS

First and foremost, the U.S. government must elevate homeland defense and civil support to a first tier priority within DOD and resource DSCA as a primary mission. In the 2009 Quadrennial Roles and Missions Review Report, *Homeland Defense and Civil Support* was listed first among the department's core mission areas.[72] However, by 2012, when DOD published *Sustaining U.S. Global Leadership: Priorities for 21st Century Defense*, "*Defend the Homeland and Provide Support to Civil Authorities*" had dropped to seventh on the department's list of primary missions.[73]

This shift in emphasis was not inadvertent. It reflected a deliberate and deeply disturbing shift in DOD policy. The fundamental principles of war rarely, if ever, change. However, war is subject to constant shifts in technology and its application. In the 21st century, the easy transportability of CBRNE weapons has fundamentally changed the character of conflict, making asymmetric warfare employing such weapons a threat that is almost undetectable. Associating this asymmetric CBRNE threat with any particular terrorist organization (e.g., al-Qaeda) or nation state (e.g., Iran) would be a serious mistake. This form of warfare is available to all of America's potential adversaries, and intends to produce strategic results. Some senior U.S. military leaders understand the fundamental nature of this change, but many do not. Some believe that homeland defense and civil support should be at the top of DOD's priority list, while others are comfortable listing it seventh. Going forward, it is essential to understand homeland defense and civil support as integrated elements of DOD's larger operational framework. A holistic approach to 21st-

---

[72]U.S. Department of Defense, "Quadrennial Roles and Missions Report," January 2009, p. 5, http://www.defense.gov/news/jan2009/qrmfinalreport_v26jan.pdf (accessed January 2013).

[73]U.S. Department of Defense, "Sustaining U.S. Global Leadership: Priorities for 21st Century Defense," January 2012, p. 5, http://www.defense.gov/news/Defense_Strategic_Guidance.pdf (accessed September 2012).

century security will require changes in professional military education, sustained engagement by senior civilian officials at the Pentagon, close congressional oversight, blunt statutory direction, and, ultimately, informed presidential leadership.

Strengthening National Guard (CST/CERFP/HRF) force structure at the state level to ensure that DOD has a robust and reliable DSCA capacity that can rapidly and effectively respond to domestic catastrophic disasters is the number one recommendation of this monograph. DOD identified this in its Strategy for *Homeland Defense and Civil Support*: The Department of Defense will be prepared to provide forces and capabilities in support of domestic CBRNE consequence management, with an emphasis on preparing for multiple, simultaneous mass casualty incidents. DOD's responses will be planned, practiced, and carefully integrated into the national response.[74]

Seven years later DOD still cannot deliver on that promise. USNORTHCOM has too few troops with too little equipment and insufficient field training. An increased effort to focus National Guard capabilities must be addressed by DOD. The necessary corrections should be implemented within a framework that ensures the identified CBRNE response forces are: 1) considered national assets, 2) are under presidential command and control, 3) assigned to USNORTHCOM, and 4) trained and equipped with sufficient operational mass and capability.

As a result to the consistent leadership of the National Guard and continuous mission refinement, the governors now possess robust Title 32 CBRNE response capabilities, sufficient to address any foreseeable mid-range CBRNE event. However, if a complex catastrophe were to occur—especially a series of simultaneous mass casualty CBRNE attacks—the most likely course of action would also be the most dangerous. USNORTHCOM's only standing DCRF would be

---

[74]U.S. Government Accountability Office, "U.S. Northern Command Has a Strong Exercise Program, but Involvement of Interagency Partners and States Can Be Improved," (Washington, D.C.: U.S. Government Accountability Office, September 2009), 3.

fully committed to the first CBRNE event. Thereafter, poorly trained general utility forces would fill the requirements as additional response forces, subject to the authority and direction of operational command elements that still exist largely on paper. For these additional forces responding to multiple near simultaneous catastrophes, a lack of training and equipment and complete lack of unit cohesion would almost certainly result in unnecessary loss of life.

The requirement exists for the USNORTHCOM commander, deputy commander, all principal deputies, the Army North commander, and the DCRF commander to be experienced in planning and executing DSCA missions. USNORTHCOM is not the place for on-the-job training. The Senate Armed Services Committee should address in the future that no officer nominated for command of USNORTHCOM will be deemed qualified for confirmation unless that officer has a demonstrated history of significant experience and superior professional performance in the execution of civil support or humanitarian assistance operations. The selection of qualified National Guard and Reserve Component officers for active-duty command and principal staff assignments at all levels of USNORTHCOM's force structure should become routine.

When assessing USNORTHCOM's identified requirements, the Secretary of Defense should consistently emphasize the improvement of operational capabilities. In the aftermath of a domestic catastrophic event, DOD's ability to quickly execute its DSCA missions in support of civil authorities could mean the difference between a contained situation and massive casualties. The anticipated casualties associated with the fifteen National Planning Scenarios make it clear that this is especially true in the event of a CBRNE attack. To respond to such an event, USNORTHCOM needs the right people in sufficient numbers, properly trained with the necessary equipment, ready to rapidly execute operational plans that have already been rigorously tested in a realistic field-training environment. With the safety of the American people being uncertain, it should be the number one priority of the U.S. government to fund all identified gaps in capabilities at the local state level.

44

BIBLIOGRAPHY

Academic Papers

Austin, Joseph. "Defense Support of Civil Authorities – Are We Organized Right?," Carlisle Barracks, Pennsylvania: U.S. Army war College, March 2007.

Beckler, Mark M. "Insurrection Act Restored: States Likely to Maintain Authority Over National Guard in Domestic Emergencies," Fort Leavenworth, Kansas: School of Advance Military Studies, May 2008.

Heyer, Robert. "Introduction to CBRNE Terrorism: An Awareness Primer and Preparedness Guide for Emergency Responders," Monograph Series, Longmont, CO: Disaster Preparedness and Emergency Response Association, 2006.

Murtha, Anthony. "DSCA Surveying Institutional Challenges," Fort Leavenworth, Kansas: School of Advance Military Studies, May 2009.

Taylor-Powell, Ellen and Marcus Renner. *Analyzing Qualitative Data*, University of Wisconsin-Extension: Cooperative Extension Publishing Operations, 2003.

Articles

Harkin, Jan B. ed., "Transforming the National Guard and Reserves Into a 21st Century Operational Force," *Defense, Security and Strategies Journal*, Nova Science Pub Inc, 2010.

Hilburn, Matt."Joint Army/Marine Corps Counterinsurgency Center Aims to 'Change the Mindset' of Military Strategy: Rethinking the Enemy," *Sea Power*, April 2007.

Jacobs, MG Jeffrey A. "CCMRF and Use of Federal Forces in Civil Support Operations," *Army Magazine*, Association of U.S. Army, July 2009.

Nelms, Jordan."Equipment Standardization," *Domestic Preparedness Journal* (March 2012).

McAteer, Beth."Finding Bed in the Middle of the Disaster," *Domestic Preparedness Journal* (May 2012).

Stow, Jamie. "A Helping Hand from the Defense CBRN Response Force," *Domestic Preparedness Journal* (May 2012).

Van Alstyne, Christian M. *Potential Standards and Methods for the National Guard's Homeland Response Force*, Monterey, California: February, 2012.

Davis, Lois M., Mariano, Louis T., Pace, Jennifer E., Cotton, Sarah K., Steinberg, Paul. *Combating Terrorism: How Prepared Are State and Local Response Organizations*, Santa Monica, CA: RAND Corporation, 2006.

45

Joint Regulations

Defense Support to Civil Authorities (DSCA) Handbook. Vols. GTA 90-01-20. Washington, D.C.: U.S. Government Printing Office, 2011.

Chairman of the Joint Chiefs of Staff. "Operation of the Joint Capabilities Integration and Development System," CJCS Instruction 3170.01F, Arlington, Virginia: The Pentagon. 01 March 2009.

Department of Defense. *Joint Publication 1-02, Dictionary of Military and Associated Terms.* Washington D.C.: Government Printing Office, November 2010.

Department of Defense. *Joint Publication 3-0, Joint Operations Incorporating Change 1.* Washington D.C.: Government Printing Office, 13 February 2008.

U.S. Army Regulations

Department of the Army. *Army Doctrine Publication 3-28 Defense Support to Civil Authorities.* Washington D.C.: Government Printing Office, August 2012.

Department of the Army. *Army Doctrine Publication 3-0 Unified Land Operations.* Washington D.C.: Government Printing Office, October 2011.

Department of the Army. *AR 220-1 Unit Status Reporting and Force Registration – Consolidated Policies.*, Washington D.C.: Government Printing Office, July 2009.

Department of the Army. *FM 101-5 Staff Organization and Operations.* Washington D.C.: Government Printing Office, May 1984.

Department of the Army. *FM 3-35 Deployment and Redeployment.* Washington D.C.: Government Printing Office, April 2010.

National Strategy Documents

Chairman, Joint Chiefs of Staff. *The National Military Strategy of the United States.* Washington, D.C., February 8, 2011.

Department of Defense. CONPLAN 3500 CBRN Response Force (DCRF). NORTHCOM, 2011.

Department of Defense Directive (DODD) 3025.12, Employment of Military Resources in the Event of Civil Disturbances, February 4, 1994.

Department of Defense Directive (DODD) 3025.18, Defense Support of Civil Authorities (DSCA), December 29, 2010.

Department of Defense. CONPLAN 3501 Defense Support to Civil Authorities. 2009.

Federal Emergency Management Administration. "Robert T. Stafford Disaster Relief and Emergency Assistance Act, as amended, and Related Authorities." FEMA. 2007 йил June.

Defense, Department of. *National Defense Strategy*. Washington, D.C., June 2010.

Defense, Department of. *Quadrennial Defense Review Report*. Washington, D.C., February 2006.

Defense, Department of. *Quadrennial Defense Review Report*. Washington, D.C., February 2010.

The White House. *National Security Strategy*. Washington, D.C., May 2010.

U.S. Government Accountability Office Reports

U.S. Government Accountability Office. "DoD Can Enhance Efforts to Identify Capabilities to Support Civil Authorities during Disasters", Washington, D.C.: U.S. Government Accountability Office, June 2008.

U.S. Government Accountability Office. "Enhanced Leadership, Capabilities, and Accountability Controls Will Improve the Effectiveness of the Nation's Preparedness, Response, and Recovery System", Washington, D.C.: U.S. Government Accountability Office, September 2006.

U.S. Government Accountability Office. "First Responders' Ability to Detect and Model Hazardous Releases in Urban Areas is Significantly Limited", Washington, D.C.: U.S. Government Accountability Office, June 2008.

U.S. Government Accountability Office. "Homeland Defense And Weapons of Mass Destruction Additional Steps Could Enhance the Effectiveness of the National Guard's Life-Saving Response Forces", Washington, D.C.: U.S. Government Accountability Office, December 2011.

U.S. Government Accountability Office. "U.S. Northern Command Has Made Progress but Needs to Address Force Allocation, Readiness Tracking Gaps, and Other Issues", Washington, D.C.: U.S. Government Accountability Office, June 2008.

U.S. Government Accountability Office. "U.S. Northern Command Has a Strong Exercise Program, but Involvement of Interagency Partners and States Can Be Improved." Washington, D.C.: U.S. Government Accountability Office, September 2009.

Internet Sources

Army National Guard, National Guard "Fact Sheet." http://www.arng.army.mil/SiteCollectionDocuments/Publications/News%20Media%20Factsheets/ARNG_Factsheet_May_06%20ARNG%20fact%20Sheet.pdf (accessed January 2013).

Army National Guard, "National Guard CERFP Teams."
http://www.arng.army.mil/News/publications/fs/2010/Subject_papers/ National%
20Guard%20 CERFP%20Teams.pdf (accessed January 2013).

Barnett, Patrick A. "Domestic Operational Law Handbook for Judge Advocates," U.S.
Department of Defense, Directive 3025.18, December 29, 2010,
http://www.dtic.mil/whs/directives/corres/pdf/302518p.pdf (accessed January 2013).

Bill of Rights Defense Committee (BORDC). Public Law 109-364, the "John Warner Defense
Authorization Act of 2007," (H.R.5122) http://www.bordc.org/threats/hr5122.php
(accessed January 2013).

Center for Army Lessons Learned. "Operations Other than War Volume II," Disaster Assistance
Newsletter 93-6. 1993 йил October. http://call.army.mil/products/newsltrs/93-
6/chap2.html (accessed September 2012).

Commerce National Oceanic and Atmospheric Administration National Marine Fisheries Service
U.S., Department of. *Report To Congress On The Impacts Of Hurricanes Katrina, Rita,
And Wilma*, http://www.nmfs.noaa.gov/msa2007/docs/Fisheries_Report_Final.pdf
(accessed December 2012).

Defense Support to Civil Authorities (DSCA) Handbook. *Tactical Level Commander and Staff
Toolkit 2011*, http://www.survivalebooks.com (accessed November 2012).

Defense Support to Civil Authorities. Online Instruction Module. 2010. www.dsca.army.mil
(accessed September 2012).

Defense, U.S. Department of. "Sustaining U.S. Global Leadership: Priorities for 21st Century
Defense," January 2012, p. 5, http://www.defense.gov/news/Defense_Strategic_
Guidance.pdf (accessed September, 2012).

Defense, U.S. Department of. "Quadrennial Roles and Missions Report," January 2009,
http://www.defense.gov/news/jan2009/qrmfinalreport_v26jan.pdf (accessed January
2013).

Department of the Army. *Army Posture Statement (APS), "Defense CBRNE Response Force
(DCRF)," (information paper) July 2011,
https://secureweb2.hqda.pentagon.mil/VDAS_ArmyPostureStatement/2011/information_
papers/PostedDocument.asp?id=258 (accessed November 2012).

Domestic Preparedness Journal. "Weapons of Mass Destruction – Civil Support Teams," (May
2012), http://c21.maxwell.af.mil/wmd-cst.htm (accessed September 2012).

Federal Emergency Management Agency. "Hurricane Sandy Timeline,"
http://www.fema.gov/hurricane-sandy-timeline (accessed January 2013).

Hamilton, Alexander. The Library of Congress, "Federalist Papers," Federalist 8,
http://thomas.loc.gov/home/histdox/fedpapers.html (accessed January 2013).

Homeland Response Force, "Fact Sheet." http://www.defense.gov/news/d20100603hrf.pdf
(accessed December 2012).

Homeland Security, Department of. "Military Support of Civil Authorities," A New Focus for a New Millenium. 2000 йил October. http://homelandsecurity.org/journal/articles/lawlor.htm (accessed December 2012).

Homeland Security, Department of. *Presidential Directive 5.* "Management of Domestic Incidents," http://www.dhs.gov/xabout/laws/gc_1214592333605.shtm (accessed November 2012).

Homeland Security, Department of. *Presidential Directive 21.* "Public Health and Medical Preparedness," www.dhs.gov/xabout/laws/gc_1219263961449.shtm (accessed December 2012).

Homeland Security, Department of. "National Preparedness Guidelines," http://www.dhs.gov/national-preparedness-guidelines (accessed December 2012).

Jean, Grace V. "National Guard Chief: Our Weaknesses Are Here At Home," National Defense Magazine, September 2010, http://www.nationaldefensemagazine.org/archive/2010/September/Pages/OurWeaknesses AreHereAtHome.aspx (accessed Novembwer 2012).

National Response Framework Core. "National Response Plan, January 2008". www.dhs.gov/nrf_core (accessed November 2012).

RAND Corporation. "Advisory Panel on Department of Defense Capabilities for Support of Civil Authorities After Certain Incidents," Meeting Minutes, September 2009, http://www.rand.org/content/dam/rand/www/external/nsrd/DOD-CBRNE-Panel/panel/meetings/20100602/20100602-meeting-minutes.pdf (accessed January 2013).

Robinson, Spencer W. "The Role of the Army National Guard in the 21st Century; Peacekeeping Vs. Homeland Security," The National Guard Association of the United States. http://www.ngaus.org/sites/default/files/pdf/primer%20fin.pdf (accessed January 2013).

The Associated Press. *Obama signs emergency declaration for N.J. ahead of Hurricane Sandy,* http://www.nj.com/news/index.ssf/2012/10/obama_signs_emergency_declarat.html (accessed January 2013).

The Heritage Foundation. "The Role of the National Guard in Homeland Security: Heritage Foundation," http://www.heritage.org/about/staff/departments/douglas-and-sarah-allison-center-for-foreign-policy-studies (accessed December 2012).

Thompson, Donald F. "Terrorism and Domestic Response: Can DOD Help Get it Right?," *Joint Force Quarterly* 40, 1st Quarter 2006, 17, http://www.ndu.edu/inss/Press/jfq_pages/edition/i40/i40.pdf (accessed September 2012).

Tyszkiewicz, Mary T. *Journal of Homeland Security and Emergency Management,* Volume 9, Issue 1 Article 32, http://www.journalhsdemer.org/adapt (accessed January 2013).

United States Army Combined Arms Center. "Joint Task Force-Civil," (information paper), http://usacac.army.mil/cac2/call/docs/10-16/ch_6.asp (accessed November 2012).

United States Northern Command. "U.S. Northern Command's Support to Hurricane Sandy,"
http://www.northcom.mil/News/2012/102912.html (accessed January 2013).

U.S. NORTHCOM. "Chemical, Biological, Radiological, Nuclear and High Yield Explosive
(CBRNE) Consequence Management Response Force (CCMRF)," 2011 Army Posture
Statement. Office of the Director of the Army Staff Executive Strategy Group. July 2011.
https://secureweb2.hqda.pentagon.mil/VDAS_ArmyPostureStatement/2011/information_
papers/PostedDocument.asp?id=261 (accessed March 2012).